Dr Jones'

My gift to yo

your friend —

[signature]

Pour
for
More

RECEIVING GOD'S GRACE

JACKIE BEAVERS
WITH DICK PARKER

POUR FOR MORE
published by Looking Glass Books, Decatur, Georgia

Copyright © 2002 Jackie Beavers

Cover art and interior illustrations by Jody Hoffman
Cover design by Ron Moore

Unless otherwise indicated, Scripture quotations are from
The Holy Bible, New King James Version (NKJV) © 1982
by Thomas Nelson, Inc.
The New International Version (NIV) © 1985
by The Zondervan Corporation

Manufactured in the United States of America

ISBN 1-929619-07-3

www.pourformore.com

To my sons, Curt and Wade, in whom I am well pleased;
my daughters-in-law, Lori and Ree, who have been better
to me than seven sons;
and my grandchildren, Trey, Morgan, Hope, Anna, Zach,
and Wade Jr., the glory of my old age.

No life is complete without the pouring and receiving
of others. I am particularly grateful for David
Beavers, into whom and from whom I have poured
and received more than any other person;
and Joan Eller, whose gift of mercy has allowed me to
stay in the race.

CONTENTS

PREFACE

*"You are the light of the world. A city that is set
on a hill cannot be hidden. Nor do they light a
lamp and put it under a basket, but on a
lampstand, and it gives light to all who are in the
house. Let your light so shine before men that
they may see your good works and glorify your
father in heaven."*

(MATTHEW 5:14-16)

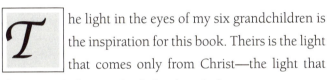 he light in the eyes of my six grandchildren is the inspiration for this book. Theirs is the light that comes only from Christ—the light that shines in darkness, the light that darkness cannot overcome (John 1:5). In their eyes gleams a celebration of life that comes only from having entered this world through a mother and a father who are each individually committed to God, to each other, and to them.

By contrast, darkness came so close to wiping out my family like a tidal wave nearly twenty-five years ago, I know the joy we experience today is nothing short of miraculous. Any sociologist who put my sons and me on a statistics sheet in 1978 would have concluded that we were destined to be at the mercy of the streets. God and I are the only ones who know the miracle my grandchildren's lives reflect, the only ones who can see how far our family has come in just one generation through the power of the cross healing to the depth of our woundedness.

I have written our story to remind future generations that God stepped into my life and changed *their* lives by giving me the strength to stop the cycle of abuse I had experienced. By their fruits those future generations will be known. By their roots they will be understood. Some of the roots of my childhood I share not to place blame or gain sympathy, but to testify to the right we have to change our destiny in Christ. Not only did He give me the power to stop the abuse, He also fulfilled his promise: "I will repay you for the years the locusts have eaten" (Joel 2:25).

I am reminded of that promise and God's fulfillment every time I see the light in the eyes of my grandchildren.

Pour
for
More

RECEIVING GOD'S GRACE

Relinquishment

The wife of a man from the company of the prophets cried out to Elisha, "Your servant my husband is dead, and you know that he revered the LORD. But now his creditor is coming to take my two boys as his slaves."
Elisha replied to her, "How can I help you?

(2 KINGS 4:1-2A)

y doctor took out his pen and prescription pad. I couldn't read the Greek he wrote, but I knew what the words meant. *Victim.*

He was sentencing me to live the rest of my life as the victim of age, high cholesterol, and whatever else he had found wrong with me when he hooked me up to his machines. He recommended a daily dose of medications to control my cholesterol. Pills would be the easiest way to keep it in check.

"Not yet," I said.

I wasn't ready to be a victim again, allowing outside influences to control my destiny. I didn't want to take the "easy" way out. I asked for three months to reregulate myself my way—God's way. If the numbers weren't satisfactory when I returned, then I would go on the pills. My doctor was skeptical. My triglycerides were well over 500—stroke and heart attack zone—and my overall cholesterol was over 800. At age fifty-nine, I was a prime candidate for what they call EDS, "early death syndrome." Diet and exercise could help and were a necessary aspect of my overall regimen, but stronger measures would still be required. I began to pray.

Twenty-four hours in a hospital cardiac care unit hooked up to an EKG machine gave me lots of time to pray and to think, not in a sense of fear or morbidity, but in contemplation. If I died today, I asked myself and God, what would I leave unfinished? The answer came almost immediately. I had some writing to do. I could not leave this world without making a permanent record of God's faithfulness in my life. But I had never written a book, and I didn't know where to start.

When I arrived home from the hospital and checked my answering machine, I heard a message from Dick Parker, a writer and friend who had heard me tell my story months earlier at a prayer retreat. In his message Dick said, "I think God is leading me to help you write your story." God's provision is always there when the time is right.

Immediately I called Dick back, and soon we were putting pen to paper.

Like the proverbial iceberg, my story encompassed more than Dick had heard at the retreat—more than I had revealed to anyone, and even more than I had confessed to my Lord. Through the process of writing this book, I brought before God long-held feelings of bitterness, anger, and fear and poured them out before Him. Only then did I realize that these bottled-up sins had been literally killing me.

The first draft was complete by the end of the three months I had bargained for, and I returned to my doctor for a follow-up examination. I had lost more than twenty pounds, and my once-deadly high cholesterol was below 200. Some of the improvement I can attribute to a change in diet and exercise. But something much bigger than a few simple lifestyle changes occurred in those ninety days. I had searched the dusty shelves deep inside myself and found vessels filled with all sorts of other negative emotions that I had tucked away like little jars of poison, ready to spill at a moment's notice. One by one, I pulled them out and poured them down the drain, then I prayed for God to refill the empty places with His love. If I had left them empty, they soon would have been filled with more and worse spirits: "Then it goes and brings along seven other spirits more evil than itself, and they enter and live there; and the last state of that person is worse than the first" (Matthew 12:45). God answered my prayer and re-filled me with His goodness, and now I am entering a new phase of life renewed by His strength.

You too may be missing out on God's blessings because you haven't made room in your spirit for them. This lesson is as old as the Old Testament and as true today as it was then: We must pour out—empty ourselves of all desires except our desire for Him—so God can refill us with His highest and best.

CLAIMING GOD'S PROMISE

Nearly twenty-five years ago I learned about pouring from the story about the prophet Elisha and a widow told in 2 Kings 4:1-7. I've been pouring ever since. When I read the first verse of the story, I immediately felt an identity with the widow.

> *The wife of a man from the company of the prophets cried out to Elisha, "Your servant my hus-*

*band is dead, and you know that he revered the
LORD. But now his creditor is coming to take my
two boys as his slaves."*

What a sad victim she was! Her husband, though a
godly man, owed so much money when he died that their
two sons were going to be sold into slavery to pay his
debts. They lived in a culture where there was nothing
legal or moral a woman could do to earn enough money,
so her options were limited. She could turn to immoral
means, or she could lock her doors and try to fend off her
creditors, or she could take her boys and run away. She
chose a fourth option. She went to the prophet Elisha, a
spokesman for God, to request help from the Lord.

I knew exactly how the widow felt. My husband had
not died, but several months before I read the widow's
story, he had filed for divorce and bankruptcy. I no longer
owned anything. Even my wedding and engagement rings
became property of the court. My two sons and I were left
destitute, and I had no marketable skills to survive. The
only thing I knew was that I was unwilling for my sons to
be enslaved by financial bondage.

Curt was thirteen years old at the time, and Wade

was ten, and the only place I could think to go was my parents' one-room fishing cabin on Lake Sidney Lanier north of Atlanta.

What a long drive it was—only fifty miles on the odometer, but a passage into a frightening new world. Up to that point my husband, through his family's business, had provided for us a beautiful home in one of Atlanta's most affluent neighborhoods. Both of our boys attended private school. Beyond the physical trappings of success, I had wonderful friends and was enjoying the fruits of a Bible study I had been leading for more than a decade.

Now the boys were leaving their school. We all were leaving our friends and familiar neighborhood, and I had not figured out how I would put food on the table.

I felt abandoned by my husband and by God. For thirteen years I had lived and breathed by the Word of God. I kept a Bible on the seat of my car, another on the kitchen counter, one in the bathroom, and one by the bed. Scripture was more than oxygen to me, and I didn't understand why my commitment had not protected me from these circumstances.

As I drove with the boys out of the city and up the highway, I knew in my head that God had said, "I will never leave you or forsake you" (Hebrews 13:5). But in my heart I felt all alone.

"Why me, God?" I cried out in my silent prayer. "Don't You know I have dedicated everything to You? Why have You cast me adrift? What about my neighbor—the one carrying on that adulterous affair? What about her, God? Why am I being punished instead?"

I heard no reply.

THE BEST JOB I COULD FIND WAS SELLING PAINT in nearby Gainesville earning minimum wage. The money didn't go far, but most months we squeaked by. We were making new friends at our new church, and several of them made discrete contributions to our cupboard. Through its youth program our church also provided an environment for my boys that I could not have given them for any amount of money. Curt and Wade joined the handbell choir, got involved in athletics, went on trips, made friends, and saw positive role models. God was providing for my family in His way even when we had nothing.

Then came the night when we were down to our last twenty dollars with three weeks until payday. Although still frustrated with God for leaving us in our precarious situation, I continued to pray and read the Bible daily. It offered my only hope. I brought the boys together to pray beside me and claim the promise in Psalm 34:10, "Those

When the student is ready, the teacher will appear.

who diligently seek Him shall not lack any good thing." We more than diligently sought God that night.

A few days later I came across the story of the widow's oil in 2 Kings 4:1-7. Her situation was so much like mine, I was eager to see how she turned out. I jumped to the end.

The man of God . . . said, "Go, sell the oil and pay your debts. You and your sons can live on what is left."

Wow! She ended up with enough to pay back her creditors and live off the rest. Here was great news! Here was *hope*! I was more than willing to study her story so I could apply her lesson to my own life.

I read the story again and again until I had virtually etched it into my memory.

*The wife of a man from the company of the prophets cried out to Elisha, "Your servant my husband is dead, and you know that he revered the L*ORD*. But now his creditor is coming to take my two boys as his slaves."*

Elisha replied to her, "How can I help you? Tell me, what do you have in your house?"

"Your servant has nothing there at all," she said, "except a little oil."

Elisha said, "Go around and ask all your neighbors for empty jars. Don't ask for just a few. Then go inside and shut the door behind you and your sons. Pour oil into all the jars, and when each is filled, put it to one side."

She left him and afterward shut the door behind her and her sons. They brought the jars to her, and she kept pouring. When the jars were full, she said to her son, "Bring me another one."

But he replied, "There is not a jar left." Then the oil stopped flowing.

She went and told the man of God, and he said, "Go, sell the oil and pay your debts. You and your sons can live on the rest."

The widow chose not to become a victim of her circumstances, but rather to overcome them with God's help. I decided to follow her example.

CREDENTIALS OF A VICTIM

I had been the "victim of victims." My parents, victims themselves, taught me the fine art of laying the blame for all my troubles at the feet of uncontrollable circumstances—usually other people. I reveal this part of my life not to claim my right to be a victim, but to show the tremendous healing power of Christ through forgiveness.

We either study our family history or we repeat it.

My mother and father fought constantly, each determined to "out victim" the other. The oldest of five children, my father was the child of a violent alcoholic father and constantly in life-threatening situations to protect his mother and siblings. My mother as a teenager was raped, and she lived the rest of her life out of rage, hatred, and shame, never able to find healing.

Later, an out-of-wedlock conception and unsuccessful abortion attempts allowed me to be born as an unwelcome intruder in their hostile world. In those pre-World War II years, pregnancy outside of marriage meant public disgrace, so my parents told their family and friends that they had been secretly married. Then, unwilling to accept the role of parents, they sent me to live with my grandparents for the first five years of my life. When I entered first grade, my parents took me back into their home. But because hurt people hurt people, I became my parents' victim.

I have no positive childhood memories with my parents, and I don't remember their ever telling me, "I love you." I often wondered why God had given me parents who obviously didn't want me. I responded by becoming performance oriented—an overachiever both in school and in my spiritual life—determined to earn the love and acceptance that I craved. Almost everything I did in life was done out of fear of abandonment. Somehow I would earn the right to be alive. Despite good grades, popularity, awards, jobs, doing good, being good, and always striving, I never quite hit the mark. Every day I awoke alone and empty with the thought, *Maybe today I'll make it if I try hard enough.*

I found sanctuary at Druid Hills Baptist Church in Atlanta and at age nine was inspired by God's message, delivered by the Rev. Louie D. Newton, to dedicate my life to Christ. I immediately became an avid reader of the Bible, with a hunger that grew out of a famine for truth. I fell in love with the church and the kindness shown me there. Every Sunday I bore out the truth of the Psalmist, "I was glad when they said to me, 'Let us go into the house of the Lord.' " Still, emptiness gnawed away at me.

At age seventeen I began dating a young man from a good family. My mother told me it was time to get married or move out on my own, and I was not strong enough to stand up against her. I always followed her orders, and a year later I was glad to move out of the hellhole of my childhood.

NOT ONLY DO WE REAP WHAT WE SOW, but when two people become one in marriage, each becomes a reaper of what the other partner has sown. Only now do I understand the invisible wind that blew against our marriage from the beginning. As one who had been abandoned and rejected, I carried into the marriage spirits that lusted to be fulfilled in any and every relationship. Until they heal, we who have been abandoned carry those spirits into every relationship. My husband brought his own baggage into our marriage, and together we reaped sorrow and disappointment. Freedom could be found only in consciously releasing those spirits and seeking forgiveness. We did not take that step, and after seven years our commitment lay in ruins.

MY FIRST PRAYER OF RELINQUISHMENT

THE WIDOW NEVER ANSWERED ELISHA'S QUESTION, "How can I help you?" Instead she let him provide the appropriate solution. How unlike us she was in that regard! When we pray to God to fix our problems, we not only lay the problem before Him, but the answer as well.

In 1967 I filed for divorce. Our three-year-old son Curt was ill, and the doctor prescribed sunshine as a part of his course of treatment, so I took him to Florida for a few days and checked us into a hotel. Our six-month-old son Wade stayed at home with his father. When we arrived at the hotel, the management informed us that several rooms had been burglarized. Fearful for our safety, I double-bolted our door, put Curt to bed, and crawled into bed myself with a book given to me by a friend. It was *Beyond Our Selves* by Catherine Marshall. Reading a spiritual book was not on my list of favorite things in those days, but I thumbed through the pages and stopped at a chapter where the author was discussing her long-term illness, her many prayers for healing, and God's apparent lack of response. She finally gave up.

> *I came to the point of abject acceptance. "I'm tired of asking" was the burden of my prayer. "I'm beaten, finished. God, You decide what You want for me for the rest of my life. . . ."*

At the point of her relinquishment, having no faith and expecting nothing in return for having given her sick self to God, her tears flowed.

> *The result was as if windows had opened in heaven; as if some dynamo of heavenly power had begun flowing, flowing into me. From that moment my recovery began.*

Though Catherine Marshall felt she had nothing worth giving, she had given the little she had to God. The principle behind her prayer of relinquishment, she explained, was like a child who brings a broken toy to his father to fix, then interrupts him with instructions on *how* to fix it. For months she had been telling God how to fix her problem, but the father can work more quickly and easily if the child relinquishes the toy, makes no attempt to interfere, and sits quietly waiting.

God began healing her when she gave up, turned her life over to Him, and stopped telling Him how she wanted it fixed. As I read those lines, something clicked inside of me. Until that moment my picture of God was of someone in charge of the moon and the stars. He had a list of my good deeds and my bad deeds—He was good, I was bad. Suddenly I was faced with a personal God who was interested in the details of my life—and I could not imagine why. I had made such a mess of things!

At that moment I literally fell on my face on the hotel carpet and cried out to God, "If You want control of my life, take it! You can have it, although I don't know what You want with it."

The feeling I experienced was one of being emptied. I was pouring myself out before God with the understanding that He would refill me with something infinitely better—like emptying a pitcher of rank, muddy water and refilling it with cool, clear spring water. Jesus said, "The water I shall give will become a fountain of water springing up into everlasting life" (John 4:14).

I don't know how long I lay there, but when I stood up I felt deep in my heart that I must drop the divorce. I called my husband and stopped the proceedings. The next day I got on a plane and flew back to Atlanta, and when I arrived home the flowers in my garden looked brighter to me. The birds'

Let the peace of God rule in your hearts.
—Colossians 3:15

songs sounded sweeter. The peace I experienced confirmed that I had made the right decision. Although the marriage did not improve, it remained intact legally for thirteen more years while God equipped me to be a single parent.

His Promise Fulfilled

I didn't dare tell anyone what I had experienced, fearing they might think I had gone off the deep end. A few weeks later, however, I heard an Atlanta woman give her testimony while speaking at our church, and I knew that what had happened to me had also happened to her. Arthritis had virtually paralyzed this woman, Julia Bridges, before she checked into the Warm Springs Clinic, where President Franklin D. Roosevelt had been treated years earlier.

"I don't believe there has ever been anyone more miserable, more disheartened, more lost, or sorrier for one's self than I was," Julia recalled. "I was without hope, without purpose, without plans, and truly without any desire to live. Though I believed I was a Christian and knew about God, I didn't know Him. It makes a vast difference."

A friend came to visit her at Warm Springs, and Julia poured out her troubles, her frustrations, and her sense of hopelessness. Her friend led Julia in a prayer of relinquishment to make room for God's divine healing. Although Julia's arthritis never completely left her, she put away her wheelchair and walked unaided until her death thirty-two years later. "The peace that only God can give has transformed my life and the lives of my household in a completely miraculous way," Julia said.

That was the transformation I believed I was experiencing, and I could hardly restrain myself from jumping across the pews to talk to her. We spoke, and Julia invited me to attend a weekly Bible study she was leading in her home. For the next several years, I sat every Monday morning drinking in the Word spoonful upon spoonful as fast as I could swallow it.

Building on the momentum Catherine Marshall's

words had created in me, I felt my spiritual strength growing. After two years of Julia's feeding, I stood looking out my dining room window one morning and thought, *If I could ask God for one thing, what would it be?* Instantly came the answer: *To communicate the message of God's love and forgiveness to even one person as Julia has to me.* I had never told anyone about His love, and I longed for the confidence to do so. Immediately, though, the enemy was there using my own thoughts to accuse me: *You've got to be kidding! Who do you think you are? Who's going to look at your messed up life and then listen to one thing you have to say about anything—especially God!*

Immediately the little flame was drowned in an ocean of doubt.

Three days later a friend, Forrest Nutting, called and said she had been diagnosed with a chronic disease. Doctors told her they had done all they could; she would have to control the stress that had led to the disease.

"For the past two years," Forrest told me, "I've seen a difference in you. The only word I know to explain it is *peace*. I was wondering if I came to your house, would you be willing to tell me how you found that peace?"

"Well, sure," I stammered. "Come on over if you like."

I didn't recognize this as the answer to my prayer. Instead, I hung up the phone and steadied myself against the counter while fear that I could neither explain nor control rushed through me. My *friend* was crossing boundaries she had no right to cross—violating my privacy! What right did she have to question my deepest thoughts?

I did not yet realize that God was already calling on me to pour out to others what He was pouring into me. He had blessed me, then He immediately transformed me into an instrument for sharing more blessings to others.

I wasn't ready for that. What if Forrest disagreed with my "simple" message? She would be rejecting me. She came the next day, and I held back. I told her I had found my peace by reading some religious books and going to church. Maybe she could do the same thing. She went home and that was that . . . until I went to bed and tossed and turned all night. I had let down my friend and my Savior by not telling her what Christ had given me in that hotel room— a peace that I could not understand or explain. The next morning I called Forrest and said, "If you'll come back, I think I can give you some answers you might be looking for."

She did come back, and I told her how I had come to know Christ in a personal way. In telling her about

Christ, I could feel the "pouring out" of myself and the refilling of my spirit with Christ's living water. Before she left my house that day, Forrest prayed to receive Christ and began the process of her pouring and God's refilling.

She also asked if I would come to her house and teach her the Word the way Julia had been teaching me. I had never taught before, but buoyed by our experience together, I told her I would. That weekend at a neighborhood party, another friend said, "I understand you're teaching a Bible study next week."

"No, I'm not!" I insisted, because I felt totally intimidated by my friend's life, which epitomized my picture of happiness. She was a beautiful woman with a loving husband and wonderful children. She had a Bible degree and taught at one of Atlanta's most prestigious private schools, and I was afraid she would see my flaws.

"Well, I would like to come," she said.

"If you're there, I won't be, because I don't have anything to teach that you don't already know!" I said in all honesty.

Despite my rudeness, my friend was in Forrest's living room on Monday morning, along with twenty other women waiting to hear what I had to say. I poured out my pride and proceeded with a lesson on John 15: Jesus is the vine, and we are the branches. As I opened my mouth, I was aware that God was teaching through me. After the session, my friend came to me and said, "Jackie, when I walked through the door I didn't know it but I was on my way to hell. I don't want to walk out that way. Would you pray with me?"

I believe God had spoken to her not so much through the lesson as through my heart. People can debate scripture and theology, but they cannot deny what Christ has done in our lives.

A few months later she led her husband to the Lord, and he started a men's Bible study in Atlanta that continues to flourish today.

Before that Monday morning my self-image was that of a woman whom God had neglected when He was distributing His divine gifts. In my heart I was already as destitute as the widow who went to Elisha. But in Forrest's living room I learned that God had given me the gift of teaching, and operating out of that gift has been a great joy in my life. Our satisfaction, our prosperity, our meaning comes from operating out of His gifts, pouring out to others what He has poured into us.

Acres of Diamonds

TWO

"Tell me, what do you have in your house?"
"Your servant has nothing there at all," she said,
"except a little oil."
(2 KINGS 4:2B)

*D*espite my first prayer of relinquishment, I continued to pray that God would solve my problem my way—that He would change my husband and save our marriage. To this day I believe God's desire was that our marriage—all marriages—should thrive. But God doesn't violate human will, and my husband stood in opposition to the continuation of our marriage. So God worked through the circumstances we created to achieve His good. If only it had been so clear to me at the time.

When my husband left, I learned firsthand the fallacy of depending on the things of this world, which are here today and gone tomorrow. I had read, and even taught, the lesson of the rich young ruler who asked Jesus, "What shall I do to inherit eternal life?" (Luke 18:18).

Jesus told him, "Sell all that you have and distribute to the poor, and you will have treasure in heaven; and come, follow Me" (Luke 18:22).

Our Lord was telling him, and us, that we must stop depending on worldly wealth. Anything we depend on other than God is sin, whether it's money, a relationship, alcohol, food—anything. Even after the material things were taken away from my boys and me, I did not immediately understand this principle.

Either you trust God or you don't.

If the prophet Elisha had knocked on the door of our little cabin and asked, "How can I help you?" I would have answered, "Give us the money we need to survive." I still depended on the things of this world. I didn't understand that my problem wasn't a lack of money. It was a lack of trust—trust in God to take care of us.

I took the only job I could get, selling paint for minimum wage, and grew so filled with fear and bitterness I became physically sick. During my breaks at work I had to lie down on the bathroom floor with my face on the cool tile to regain my strength. I drove home in the afternoons to meet the boys when they arrived from school, but some days I was so sick I had to pull the car off the road and lie across the front seat for several minutes before I could continue. The bitterness was literally killing me.

I was diagnosed with a connective tissue disease, yet everything else in my life seemed disconnected. I had taken matters into my own hands, and I was failing miserably. I walked through the door into that dark little cabin and felt totally abandoned by the God I had come to trust. How many times in my life had I read Hebrews 13:5, where God states emphatically, "I will never leave you nor forsake you"?

As abandoned and alone as I felt, I continued to read the Bible and pray. I was so desperate for any help, I recited over and over, "God has not given us a spirit of fear . . ." (2 Timothy 1:7). I truly wanted to believe.

"What do you have in your house?"

I read Elisha's question to the widow and thought, "How insensitive!" She came to him broke, a victim of almost unspeakable circumstance, and the first thing he said was, "What do you have?"

I believe her focus, like mine, was not on what she had, but on what she *didn't* have. That is our natural response to tragedy. I responded to Elisha's question with a question of my own: "What in the world do I have that could help my sons and me out of this impossible situation?"

The widow saw no relationship between what she needed and what she had, and neither did I.

"Tell me, what do you have?" I felt the Holy Spirit asking me.

I drew a blank.

"Nothing?" the Spirit asked. "Look again. Go back over your life and see what you find. Draw on your roots to find your fruits."

I came to the heart of the matter: When we examine our lives closely, we will see that God has already given us what we need to get what we want. Our work is twofold: Identify His gift, then give it back to Him. Pour it out before Him, and He will multiply it abundantly.

THE WIDOW WITH THE OIL WAS NOT the only deficit thinker in the Bible. One of the most familiar statements in the New Testament is, "We have nothing but . . ."

Even Jesus' disciples were deficit thinkers. Five thousand men plus women and children had gathered to hear Jesus speak of the kingdom of God and to be healed. Toward the end of the day they became hungry, and the disciples suggested that Jesus send them home so they could eat.

"You give them something to eat," Jesus told them.

They looked around and saw nothing but their deficit. "We have nothing but five loaves and two fish," they said.

They were about to learn the lesson the widow with the

Some people just show up for the loaves and fish, while others show up and offer what they have.

oil had learned, and the lesson I had yet to learn—the lesson of God's abundance (Matthew 14:13-21).

Jesus told the disciples to bring the loaves and fish to Him. That's the way it is . . . once we identify the "little bit of oil" or the "five loaves and two fish," we must bring them to Him.

Then Jesus took one little boy's lunch, thanked God for it, broke it, and gave the pieces to the disciples. The disciples gave it to the multitudes, and they all ate and were filled. Afterward they took up twelve baskets filled with fragments that remained.

Having been trained to rely on the resources in the physical realm, I did not ask for, let alone expect, a miracle. This is not something I say with pride. I wish I could tell you that from the time I walked down the aisle at Druid Hills Baptist Church to dedicate my life to Christ, I trusted Him above all earthly things. And I wish I could say that when I fell on my face on the hotel room floor that I truly gave Christ every part of my life. But the truth

Light received brings more light. Light rejected brings darkness.

is, my surrender has been progressive—too often one step forward and two steps backward. I still hold back, even though He has transformed into magnificence every petty earthly thing I have given Him. He calls on me to pour new things out to Him every day and allow Him to shine His light into the dark corners of my self to illuminate the things I need to clean out.

ACRES OF DIAMONDS

Russell H. Conwell, founder of Temple University, was one of America's most popular public speakers in the late nineteenth and early twentieth centuries. Everywhere he went, people wanted to hear the same speech: "Acres of Diamonds."

Conwell had heard the legend of a prosperous Persian farmer who, enticed by rumors of fields of diamonds, sold his farm and searched the world for riches. Far from home, exhausted and destitute, he died a broken man. Soon after his death, diamonds were found back home on the man's own farm.

Conwell told thousands of audiences, "Your diamonds are not in faraway mountains or in distant seas; they are in your own backyard if you will but dig for them."

THE PROPHET ASKED THE WIDOW what seemed like a cruel question—"What do you have?"—because he wanted her to take the first step: to identify God's gifts to her. Seeking an answer to that question, I went back to my beginning all over again, searching for my "acres of diamonds," and soon I began to see.

For the first five years of my life, when my parents sent me away, I lived with my grandparents on their farm in rural east Georgia. Country life in the 1940s was hard, with neither electricity nor running water. Every morning somebody had to milk the cows and gather eggs. In spring my grandfather had to plant the cotton. In summer they told me to help chop that cotton. Only I didn't know chopping cotton meant chopping the weeds *around* the cotton. I wasn't much help to them. In fall Daddy Harris ran the combine—sometimes with me in his lap—picking the bursting white bolls. In winter, with only the fireplaces for warmth, we slept on mattresses my grandmother had stuffed with feathers, under quilts she had sewn.

The little farm was miles from the nearest florist, but every morning my breakfast tray was adorned with a fresh flower Mama Harris had picked from her garden and put in my favorite bud vase, which was shaped like a little dog. She also made all my clothes, after taking me to the feed store where I picked out the feed sack from which she would sew my next dress. Then she taught me how to sit in it like a lady. *Saks* or *sucks*, I didn't know the difference.

On the fourth Saturday of the month, Mama Harris opened the bottom door of the corner cupboard in the dining room and carefully unwrapped the communion cups, then placed them on silver trays to take to church the next morning. This was just the beginning of her preparation for Sunday. She also put the finishing touches on her Sunday school lesson, which she worked on though the week. Then she went out into the yard and fed the chickens—and killed one—dug potatoes, picked beans and corn, and if it was late enough in the season, apples for a pie.

On Sunday morning she rose before the sun to milk the cows, cooked ham and biscuits for breakfast, helped me get ready for church, taught Sunday school, played the piano for church, and afterward brought the preacher and half the community home for dinner at a table graced with freshly starched linen and a bouquet from the garden. In summer my grandfather churned fresh homemade ice cream, and in winter we ate fruit, nuts, and candy around the fire before returning to church for evening services. The hearth we gathered around had been whitewashed with a mixture of white clay that my grandmother and I gathered from a gully out in the woods.

By any economic standard, then or now, my grandparents lived in simplicity. In my pre-reading days I stood beside her in church singing, "We shall come rejoicing bringing in the *sheets*." The next morning Mama Harris took out the sheets; Monday was wash day, and her fingers turned red and raw from washing clothes in a bucket, wringing them out, and hanging them on the line. On her left hand she wore a smooth gold ring, which she said had been engraved with orange blossoms when she and Daddy Harris were married. It had been worn smooth over the years, leaving only the golden gleam that symbolized to me a union that would continue to gleam in a darkened world.

By faith Moses, when he became of age, refused to be called the son of Pharaoh's daughter, choosing rather to suffer affliction with the people of God than to enjoy the passing pleasures of sin.
—Hebrews 11:24-25

When I think of Mama Harris I am reminded of Jochebed, the mother of Moses. The Bible doesn't tell us how long Moses lived in his family's home before being taken to live with Pharaoh's daughter, but during those first years his mother must have been a powerful influence on him. Through the limitless love God supplied her, she showed her son that he was a child of destiny. And while she could not have foreseen that he would lead the nation out of Egypt, she displayed before him the same faith, courage, and strength that had led her to risk all by hiding him as an infant and setting him adrift in the Nile River.

Many like Jochebed have planted seeds of hope and

of love in the children they influence. Mama Harris did that for me. She also set deep within me the idea that prosperity is a state of mind, not an overflowing bank account— that the things of this world were created to meet the needs of people. She was never impressed with possessions beyond that value.

She served a God of abundance, and never operated out of a position of deficit—even when she had no money.

AFTER I MOVED INTO MY PARENTS' HOME, my third-grade teacher, Evelyn Smith, took the opportunity to sow more diamonds by expressing her love for me in every way possible, even the waif I was, and helping me to value myself. At Christmastime she gave me the role of Mary, the mother of Jesus, in the school play. From early fall until Christmas, every day we practiced that play, and every day I said my one line, "Let it be unto me according to Thy word" (Luke 1:38).

In my mind I knew only that I was saying words in a play that made me feel good to be chosen. But God was doing a much deeper work than I realized. I said those words so many times that I believe they literally carved themselves into my heart. God was planting His own acres of diamonds.

A Passion

"What do you have?" the prophet asked.

"Nothing at all except a little oil," the widow replied.

Like her, I was focusing only on the tangible things in my life, so I did not understand that I too had "a little oil." My "oil" was intangible; it was my *passion* that my sons would not be limited by financial bondage. I was totally committed to providing them with a quality education, good books to read, and the extras in life like music and other opportunities. I just didn't know how I would do it. My bucket of business knowledge or training was totally empty, and the things I wanted for my sons cost much more money than I could earn at the paint store.

I was about to learn two of the most important lessons of my life:

God always gives us what we need to get what we want.

God will take whatever we pour out to Him, whether tangible or intangible, and multiply it back to us.

My passion for my boys was just what God wanted, for He despises the lukewarm: "So, because you are lukewarm—neither hot nor cold—I am about to spit you out of my mouth" (Revelation 3:16). He will take our passion, even if it's for something other than Him, and transform it. The most such dramatic transformation was of the passionate zealot Saul of Tarsus into the passionate Apostle Paul.

The story is told of Viktor Frankl who, when released from a German concentration camp, was asked how he had survived. "If the 'why to' is strong enough, the 'how to' will come," he said. In other words, when you're passionate in your commitment to a task, you *cannot* fail, because you don't hold anything back.

Failure for my sons and me meant the streets, and that was unacceptable. I would not allow us to fail, and I knew God would not allow us to fail. That was my passion—my "why to."

God wants that same kind of passion for Him. He wants us to be able to stand with the Psalmist and say, "As the deer pants for streams of water, so my soul pants for you, O God" (42:1). While I was working on this chapter I drove by a church with a message on its sign: "The world expects our best. God commands our all!" He doesn't want a token. He doesn't want a portion. He doesn't want a tenth. He wants *everything*.

A Plan of Action

Elisha said, "Go around and ask all your neighbors for empty jars. Don't ask for just a few."
(2 KINGS 4:3)

lisha immediately put the widow's passion to work, laying out a simple, specific plan of action—yet one that appeared to have no relevance to meeting her needs. How often we see the truth of Isaiah 55:8: "'For my thoughts are not your thoughts, neither are my ways your ways,' declares the LORD." God's solution to our problems makes no sense to us. It made no sense to Abraham and Sarah when God told them He would make a nation of them though they were old and childless. It made no sense to the crowd when Christ told them, "Do not worry about your life, what you will eat or what you will drink . . ." (Matthew 6:25). It made no sense to the disciples when Christ was nailed to the cross.

But from God's perspective, it all makes perfect sense.

Elisha told the widow to borrow vessels from all her neighbors. She must have thought he was crazy; she needed money, not empty pots. But God had given the prophet a plan that met the widow's needs at many levels.

Elisha knew that the widow's first reaction to her looming disaster would be to detach herself from those around her, so he told her to connect with her neighbors. That was Step One. Separation is the definition of hell. Communion is that which removes separateness from our lives. When we allow trouble to isolate us, we deny the deepest cry of our souls.

A dream without a task is but a dream.

A task without a dream is mere drudgery.

A dream with a task is the hope of the world.

The widow had to share her pain with her neighbors. When she asked her neighbors for their vessels, she had to admit her brokenness. Asking God for help is one thing. Asking people for help is another thing altogether. It required that the woman humble herself before others, admit she could not make it alone, and risk possible ridicule.

I see this principle played out over and over: Take the first step and expose your weakness, and people will immediately move to cover you. Hide your weakness, and people will seek to expose you. When people attempt to hide their needs behind expensive clothes and cars, embarrassed to admit their financial straits, others immediately perceive their dishonesty and feel no desire to support them. On the other hand, people who are honest about their motivations are rewarded with trust.

WHEN I WAS GOING THROUGH MY DIVORCE, I remember walking up and down the aisles of the neighborhood grocery story where I had shopped for years, running into friends from *produce* to *checkout*. These same friends now turned their buggies in another direction when they saw me, leaving me hurt and ashamed. I understand better today that they just didn't know how to "be there" for me; they were embarrassed because they didn't know what to say. But hurting people don't need to be "fixed"; they just need to connect with other people. If Elisha had spoken to the widow's neighbors, I believe he would have told them to go ask her how they could help.

Acknowledging another's pain enables us to accelerate our potential in every arena. We must overcome our fear of vulnerability and reach out to the widows and any other hurting people—and everybody is hurting. We are a corporate people who serve a corporate God whose healing touch often flows from one person to another.

People need people.

God continually calls us to take the first step, whether it's from our own brokenness or to recognize and meet the needs of another.

Another Prayer of Relinquishment

The paint store was not going to ensure our well-being, so to supplement my income, I helped people with interior decorating. After a few months I was able to leave the store and decorate full time. My physical pain began to subside and I enjoyed the work, but cash flow was a series of peaks and valleys.

In my continuing depression over finances I was spilling my problems to my friend Helen Maddox, who asked, "So what's the worst thing that can happen, Jackie? You and the boys starve to death and you end up in heaven." I can't say I appreciated her long-term view, but over time it helped me overcome the fear of my immediate circumstances. In the end, no matter what, God would take care of us.

Soon I began to see His hand at work in the here and now. Grace Kinser, a friend and a great Christian matriarch in Atlanta, called one day and said, "I want you to come to my house for a few nights. I need you to do some decorating."

Grace and I both knew she didn't really need my help—she was just looking for a way to assist me financially without giving me a handout. She and her daughter Carolyn had already been putting food in my refrigerator and letting me "shop" from their closets. I accepted her offer. Perhaps in the back of my mind I also hoped Grace would offer some advice.

If you're from the South, you've seen Grace's name, "Mrs. Kinser," hundreds of times on the salads she created—chicken, ham, pimento cheese—and sold in the lunch meat cases of supermarkets. Grace began making and selling salads in the early 1950s so she could support the radio ministry of evangelist Dr. Charles Fuller. By the time I met her, she was supporting dozens of ministries with the proceeds of her multimillion-dollar company.

It was November 1978 when I drove down the highway toward Grace's house in Atlanta with rain pouring so hard I could hardly see. Inside the car the atmosphere was even gloomier. I didn't see how things would ever work out financially for us.

"God," I prayed, "Your Word tells me that You came so that I would have abundant life—a life that would bring glory and honor to Your name. But when I look at my life I see sickness, poverty, and suffering. I don't see anything about my life that would draw anybody to You. God, if this *is* the abundant life and I'm just not recognizing it, then I don't want anything else. But there's something in my spirit telling me we are not experiencing all You want for us. So my prayer is simply this: I want everything that is mine in You. I don't want anything that belongs to someone else, but I want everything that You have established as mine."

The rain continued to fall outside the car as I said *amen*, yet somehow I felt as if all of the heavy darkness inside of me had lifted. I cannot explain it, and I didn't know what was coming next, but I felt as if a heavy load had been lifted. I felt hopeful for the first time in months. Only later did I connect this experience with what was about to happen at Grace's house.

Grace got right to the point with her plan of action for me. She handed me a blue cosmetic kit and said, "Jackie, this is what you're going to do with your life. I'm going to loan you forty dollars, enough money to start this business, and you're going to sell cosmetics." This seemed as strange to me as gathering empty jars, but, as I have said, we too often do not have God's perspective. He's looking at the top side of the tapestry, with its beauty and distinct pattern, but all we see are the unrelated colors and hanging threads on the back side.

Grace Kinser could see the tapestry, at least in part, and she saw where I fit into it. For years she had been supporting the ministry of her friends Cameron and Elaine Townsend, founders of Wycliffe Bible Translators. Wycliffe has translated the Bible into more than five hundred languages and is committed to seeing that every man, woman, and child be able to read God's Word in their own language.

The Townsends' daughter Dell and her husband were students at Dallas Theological Seminary, and Dell was selling skin care products for a network marketing company to supplement their income. Grace agreed to find some-

THE WEAVER

My life is but a weaving
Between my Lord and me,
I cannot choose the colors
He worketh steadily.

Ofttimes He weaveth sorrow,
And I in foolish pride
Forget He sees the upper
And I, the underside.

Not till the loom is silent
And the shuttles cease to fly
Shall God unroll the canvas
And explain the reasons why.

The dark threads are as needful
In the Weaver's skillful hand
As the threads of gold and silver
In the pattern He has planned.
-Author Unknown

one in Atlanta to work under Dell selling the product. That's where I fit in. To give Dell double benefit, Grace signed up her daughter Carolyn directly under Dell, and me under Carolyn.

In the midst of our living in near poverty, the only thing I was sure of was that I was of no value to any person or any company. No one who enters the field of direct sales could have been less likely to succeed than I. But I still had my passion to take care of my sons. My "why to" was still strong.

My on-the-job training consisted of Grace saying, "The company will send you a box of products and contracts. Sell your product and get other people to do the same." That's all I needed—the basics of network marketing. I had witnessed the power of Grace's influence in the success of her company; now I was captivated by her remarkable gift of persuasion. She convinced me to do something I never would have dreamed, and I was ignited by her spark.

With Grace's brief instructions and tremendous influence, Carolyn and I set out in a rowboat to catch Moby Dick, and we carried the tartar sauce with us. I would love to take even an ounce of credit for the success that followed, but my fear of the Lord is too great to face the consequences of such a lie.

Operating from a Vision

With Christmas coming on, I knew women would not have time to meet with me and try the various products I could offer, so I decided to begin making sales calls after the first of the year. However, I was not about to squander two months.

Throughout the Christmas season I followed the example of the widow and told everybody I saw what I was doing. When I ran errands, went to the dry cleaner, the hairdresser, or the grocery store, I explained that I would no longer be decorating, but would be selling cosmetics instead. At Christmas parties, in church, and at my sons' school, I told everybody I knew. I recorded the name of everyone I spoke with during those two months in a small red address book that I carried in my purse.

In January I began following up on the contacts I had made the previous two months and was surprised to find that many of the women not only wanted to buy cosmetics from me, they wanted to sell with me. One of the first people I told about my new venture was my friend Jo

Shippen, and she immediately said she wanted to join me. Although Jo had never been in business, she brought a spiritual maturity and an understanding of finances and organization that I lacked. I had never balanced a checkbook in my life, so Jo's skills would be critical to my success. She took my lofty ideas and created a blueprint, then Janice Brannon joined us, bringing an ability to take Jo's blueprints and put them into action where the rubber met the road. As others joined us, all brought their unique gifts, be they speechmaking or cookie baking, and everyone poured out those gifts in order for the group to be whole.

> *A man's gift makes room for him and brings him before great men.*
> *—Proverbs 18:16*

My passion to succeed apparently was contagious. A number of the women joining me were my Atlanta friends—affluent housewives who had never experienced the joy of generating income. We quickly became a growing team—a team with an unorthodox approach to business.

Remember, this was 1979, when business people almost never discussed religion at the workplace. For my part, though, God was all I knew. My practical knowledge had come from leading a Bible study for a decade, so when a woman said she wanted to sell our product, I would ask her, "Are you a Christian? Because if you're not, let me tell you why you probably don't want to be in this business. You see, I don't know anything about business, but I'm a Christian and I have the Holy Spirit in me. So if you have the Holy Spirit in you too, then He'll work with us together to make this thing work. But if you're not a Christian, it probably won't work for you."

I knew so little about business I didn't realize how bizarre my little speech sounded—or how many federal employment rules I broke by making it. But I didn't stop there.

If the woman was married, I would ask her, "Do you have your husband's support in coming to work with us?" (I ignored the fact that we were in the height of the feminist movement.) If she answered *no*, I told her, "I don't think you should sell with us until you have your husband's support, because if it's not going to work for your family, it's not going to work for you. And if it's not going to work for you, I don't want to waste your time and mine." Then I would pray with her and ask her to get her husband's permission to work in the business before coming back.

A July 2001 article in *Fortune* magazine stated, "People who want to mix God and business are rebels. . . . They refuse to bow to the all-too-common notion that much of the work done in corporate America must be routine, dull, and meaningless; they want and expect more."

Twenty-two years before that article was published, the women who worked with me not only expected more, they demanded it. They weren't interested in the "management by objective" theory of business prevalent in those days. That tradition, upon which corporate America had thrived for decades, directed all employee efforts toward the achievement of the companies' bottom line objectives. It did not take into account the employees' goals and dreams.

I found network marketing to be a unique environment in which individual supremacy reigned and where anyone who chose could join the aristocracy of excellence. Each person earned what he or she was worth, not what the job was worth. We didn't manage them with a paycheck, but rather inspired them to achieve their own dreams.

Then one day in early 1979 Jo Shippen announced

that she had heard a wonderful speaker deliver a message titled "A Prayer to Ignite Your Life." She brought a tape of his message, and I listened to Bruce Wilkinson present what years later would become a book entitled *The Prayer of Jabez.*

God's current agenda for Jabez in the world was known only to Him.

On his tape Bruce explained how God wanted me to live an extraordinary life, and He was ready to help me achieve it. He suggested that listeners pray every day for thirty days the prayer Jabez had prayed:

"Oh, that You would bless me indeed, and enlarge my territory, that Your hand would be with me, and that You would keep me from evil, that I may not cause pain!" (1 Chronicles 4:10).

We told other women who were selling with us about the prayer, and we began to pray it every day. We were operating out of a vision. My vision was based on my passion for my boys. Other women had different visions. A woman from Athens, Georgia, came to us so shy that I knew she would never make it in sales. Then she explained why she wanted to sell cosmetics.

"There are so many small churches in north Georgia that have never had the first stained glass window," she said. "I'm going to help as many of them as I can."

God expanded His territory through that woman, and she went on to become the top salesperson in our organization. Her experience was reminiscent of Grace Kinser, who didn't even like to cook, but whose vision was to give more money to ministries. She told a local newspaper, "I just wanted to help a minister in a small way because I believed in what he was doing. When I think back to where I started, it has been one miracle after another that has happened to me."

God has placed a vision in the heart of every person—the acre of diamonds Conwell described—and He wants us to live out that vision through the plan of action He provides. When we do, our vision expands and God gives us even greater opportunities (Matthew 25:21).

In the first five years of my life, three decades before I began to work with this passionate group of women, God and my grandmother sowed a diamond deep within me. My grandmother showed me how to operate out of God's abundance, no matter how much or how little I had. With God's help, I was now plowing away the dirt I had piled on top of that glittering gem.

Behind Closed Doors

FOUR

*"Then go inside and shut the door behind you and
your sons. Pour oil into all the jars, and when
each is filled, put it to one side."*

(2 KINGS 4:4)

lisha understood that the widow's needs ran
much deeper than her apparent financial problems, and his plan of action addressed those
needs. He told her to "shut the door behind you and your
sons." She needed to deal with some issues in the privacy
of her home. Only then would God give her the faith necessary to complete His plan of action.

My family had private issues to deal with as well—
generational issues. God reminds us from the beginning
that we are a generational people and He is a generational
God. Throughout the Bible we find lists of generations—
who begot whom. The Bible also tells us that the actions
of one generation affect the generations that follow. "I, the
LORD your God, am a jealous God, visiting the iniquity of

the fathers upon the children to the third and fourth generations" (Deuteronomy 5:9). God is not threatening us with that statement but instead explaining that our actions have consequences, and the ripple effects of those consequences can continue long after we're gone.

For example, five generations of sexual perversion in David's household followed his sin with Bathsheba until Asa finally "did what was right in the eyes of the LORD . . . and banished the perverted persons from the land and removed all the idols that his fathers had made" (1 Kings 15:11, 12). David's sin did not go to the grave with him, but rather it stayed within his family until someone repented of it, renounced it, and replaced it with God's blessings.

The actions of the widow's husband—his poor financial management—led creditors to come knocking at the door to take his sons and sell them into slavery. The sons had not incurred the debt, but they would pay the price.

In my parents' home love was absent, and I could not fill the deficit left in my soul. One morning when I was a young mother, however, I experienced the true source of love and replenishment. I was carrying an armload of folded laundry up the steps, when about halfway up I was struck with the overwhelming realization that I did not possess the love that my children needed. I didn't know where the feeling came from, but I knew it was real. I stood on the steps, my stomach in knots, knowing I loved my boys with everything I had, but I could not give them what I did not have. No one had ever shown me how to love the way I knew my children—any children—deserved and needed to be loved, and I despaired for their loss.

Gripped by that feeling of pain and emptiness, I looked up toward the ceiling without even a prayer I could verbalize, and immediately in my spirit I felt God say, "You're catching on, Jackie. You're right. You don't have the love your children need. But if you will let Me love your children through you, they will be fine."

Instantly the laundry basket felt lighter. I abandoned the notion that I bore full responsibility for the love my sons experienced. I didn't have to repay the debt myself. Christ had already repaid it for me. In the space of less than a minute, I moved from fear to peace.

TICKET TO FREEDOM

"God sets the solitary in families; He brings out those who are bound into prosperity." (Psalm 68:6)

When I read that verse for the first time I knew this was the course God had laid for my life "before the foundation of the world" (Ephesians 1:4). I was to stop the cycle of abuse and victimization in my family so that my children and their children and future generations of our family after them would live in God's blessings rather than the enemy's cursings.

Understanding that God placed me in my family to be that solitaire gave purpose to my suffering as a child. The solitaire is the strongest possible diamond, able to withstand the most pressure while also reflecting the most light. The solitaire, by its nature, stands alone, continually strengthened by God the Creator.

I often share with others my understanding of Psalm 68:6 and see people set free by it. Women and men who experienced abuse similar to mine hear these words and realize that they were born into their abusive family situations not because "God must not like me," but because He needed someone to repent from a generational sin, take it to the cross, and allow Him to release His blessings once again.

The saying is true: I couldn't help the circumstances I was born into. But God empowered me to break the cycle in my family when I understood that I was not born as the accident of someone's lust—that God had a plan for my life: "Before I formed you in the womb I knew you; before you were born I sanctified you" (Jeremiah 1:5). The God who hung the stars has an individual eternal purpose for my life, and knowing that, there is no way I can discount my value.

Stopping generational sin is like the test used many years ago for patients of a mental hospital. Before dismissal a patient was placed in a closet with a stopped-up sink and the water running. The patient was given a mop and left for a period of time. If the supervisor checked back and found the patient was still mopping without having turned off the faucet, then the patient was deemed not ready for release. For years I mopped, believing that surely the next bucket would finally clean up the mess I had been born into. Only when I recognized generational sin, then confessed it, which meant I agreed with God about it, then repented of it, could I change the direction of my family.

Because I owed a debt I could not pay, He paid a debt He did not owe.

We are presented a choice of perpetuating our heritage or changing it. When we understand that God has a plan for us to be in our particular families, we see His eternal picture and submit to His design. With that step we have a purpose in life, and that purpose energizes us. Our scars become our credentials for ministering to others and leading them to Christ and out of bondage.

I have seen people by the hundreds come to this realization, kneel before God, and receive their place with dignity. "Instead of your shame you shall have double honor" (Isaiah 61:7).

PRAYERS OF A STRANGER

Sometimes God brings other people into our lives to supply the love or the faith we lack just when we need them. Wade, my younger son, developed dangerously high blood pressure at an early age, and I took him to New York every three weeks to see a specialist. About the same time I was taking Curt, our older son, to the orthodontist on a summer morning. He was wearing shorts, and the way the sunlight hit his leg as he sat beside me in the car, I saw a big lump on his knee that I knew was not "okay."

These were the days when I lived with an extremely negative attitude, and I immediately envisioned only the worst—cancer. That same year cancer had struck Edward Kennedy Jr. as a child, leading to the amputation of a leg. Anticipating the worst for Curt, I rushed him to his pediatrician, who sent us straight to a surgeon. He recommended immediate surgery, and my fears were coming to fruition.

The dentist had just pulled several of Curt's teeth in preparation for braces, so surgery was delayed until his mouth healed to avoid infection. Envisioning Curt with only one leg, I was determined to make the best of our time before the surgery, so on our next trip to New York for Wade's treatment, we stayed at the Plaza Hotel and from there took a bus to see the Statue of Liberty. Walking back to the bus with a son holding each hand, I tripped over a cardboard box Wade had accidentally kicked into my path, fell, and broke my foot. So there we were, Wade being treated for high blood pressure, Curt with a strange growth on his knee, and me with a broken foot. We hobbled back to the hotel in the August heat and found the air conditioning had failed. The temperature, and tem-

The prayer offered in faith will make the sick person well; the Lord will raise him up.
—James 5:15

pers, were rising fast, but we somehow remained calm while we waited for a doctor to come look at my foot. He taped me from my foot to above my knee, and I awoke the next morning with my leg black, blue, and throbbing.

Before we were to catch a cab to the airport the next morning, the boys found a wheelchair and rolled me into the crowded hotel coffee shop, bumping into tables, chairs, and grumpy New Yorkers. I had never been in a worse mood. I sulked while we waited for our breakfast, and both boys started jabbering with a couple at an adjacent table. Before our breakfast arrived, and it was a *long* time, that couple knew everything there was to know about us— Wade's illness, Curt's tumor and, of course, my injury.

The couple finished eating before we did, and as they stood to leave, the man stepped over to me and said, "Excuse me, but would you mind if my wife and I prayed for you and your children?"

Stunned, all I could say was, "God knows we need it. Of course!"

The man spoke to the *maitre d'*, who directed us to an empty room down the hall, and as we knelt in prayer with this couple we had just met, all I could think was, "This is the strangest thing I have ever experienced."

How often we "see through a glass darkly" (1 Corinthians 13:12 KJV).

The night before Curt went in for surgery, that wonderful couple called and prayed for us again on the phone. Later we learned that the man was president of a steel mill and a leader in an international prayer ministry. Once again, God's provision came right on time.

Despite the surgeon's concerns, the tumor was benign, and I knew in my heart that my child walked on two strong legs because God, in His compassion and mercy, had placed that couple in the Plaza Hotel coffee shop to pray and break the bonds of hell against my son in a way that I had been incapable of doing. I didn't have enough faith for Curt's leg, so God brought people to me who did have faith and could pray us through.

Would God have been less God if Curt had lost his leg? Indeed not. This was just one of those ways He used to build our faith in Him.

SHUT THE DOOR BEHIND YOU AND YOUR SONS

The prophet knew the value of family time behind closed doors. God has always worked through family lines, and the public spotlight will always reflect what did or did not happen behind closed doors, where values are caught. When values are in place, rules are unnecessary. When values are not in place, rules are unenforceable.

One of the most important lessons my sons learned early on was submission to authority. This is the essence of the first commandment, "You shall have no other gods before me" (Exodus 20:3). Even when the authority is wrong, if you submit, God honors your obedience. Of course, there is a limit to that; if the authority asks you to do something immoral or illegal, you don't do it.

Wade had a school teacher one year who should have retired five years earlier. Wade didn't like her, and she didn't like him. It was a miserable situation, and we talked about it often. I told him to approach it as a game—to honor her position if he could not honor her personality. He saw this lady become putty in his hands when he honored her position. Wade reminded me recently how many times this lesson has served him in life.

Our prisons are filled with men and women who have never learned the value of submitting to authority. They don't know that you cannot have more authority than you have yielded to. I believe Curt and Wade are leaders today because they have learned how to be servants.

I don't mean to imply that everything was easy for us when the boys were teenagers and I was starting out in business. One Sunday afternoon two weeks after Curt got his driver's license, he ran a short errand for me. I was at home getting ready to go to church when I looked out the window and saw Curt, white as a ghost, running as fast as he could to the house. He had been in a head-on collision right around the corner. No one was hurt, but both cars were totaled. Curt ran back to the accident, and I hurried there as fast as I could. When I got there, a policeman was arresting my son for leaving the scene of an accident.

Sons are a heritage from the Lord, children a reward from him. Like arrows in the hands of a warrior are sons born in one's youth.

—Psalm 127:3-4

As the officer started to put Curt in the police car, I asked, "Sir, would you please let me bring him to the police station instead of taking him in the police car?"

"How will you get him there?" he asked. "Do you have another car?"

"No, I don't," I said, "but I give you my word I will get him there in thirty minutes."

The policeman agreed, and we walked back to the house. In my desperation I dialed the senior pastor of our church ten minutes before the service was to start. Through my hysteria, I told him what had happened.

"Stay where you are," he said. "I'll have a deacon get you in five minutes, then I'll meet you at the police station."

The deacon came and drove us to the station, where our pastor was waiting outside for us. He opened the car door, looked at our ashen faces, and said the most religious thing I had ever heard: "Lighten up, folks, the last time I got put in jail was for peeing on a policeman when I was in college."

We burst out laughing and knew immediately we were going to be okay.

Then he said, "Jackie, you stay here and let me go in with Curt to take care of things." A few minutes later they came out smiling. Curt had been able to explain that he left the scene only to find me, and the charges were dropped. That experience symbolized in the hearts of my teenage sons the true nature of a pastor of the church, which is the body of Christ, and it has led them to a similar style of church leadership as adults.

Curt and Wade understood clearly that their roles were as important to our family as mine. My work was not a nine-to-five job. My schedule was erratic, and if I had to police their activities and behaviors, I could not succeed. I had to trust them to make good decisions. We didn't have a lot of rules, but our responsibilities were clear. They knew their roles, and they never let me down.

When we were behind the closed doors of our home, we always spoke the truth, and we brought everything out into the open. We had too much at stake to hide anything under the carpet. We looked problems squarely in the eye, and I told them the truth of what was happening in my business and with our finances. I was very strict with them, but I was generous in sharing the benefits of the business.

I allowed them to confront me on any issue as long as they did so with respect and as long as they understood that I had final authority. When we disagreed, we prayed about it. I was willing to have my mind changed.

My sons will tell you I failed more often than not, but they will also tell you that they never questioned my commitment and devotion to them. My friend Harriett Sulcer, whose son is younger than mine, said to Curt, "I want my son to be just like you when he grows up. Tell me what your mom did so I can do the same thing."

He answered, "She always respected us, and she always trusted us."

Harriett then reminded my son of a time when she was a dinner guest in my home, and I left my friends at the table in order to serve the boys sectioned orange slices on silver trays in their beds. It was not a big thing, but it was a fun thing that communicated the value I place on them.

Like my grandmother before me, I was sowing diamonds.

I KNEW THAT OUR PARTNERSHIP WAS WORKING one night when the telephone rang at 10:30. I was so exhausted I couldn't get up from the bed to answer. Wade, who was eleven at the time, answered the phone.

I waited for him to call me, assuming anyone calling at 10:30 would ask for me. Instead, however, I heard Wade ask, "Have you tried the toner? What about the mask?"

Obviously a customer had called with questions about her cosmetics. Wade knew how tired I was, and rather than call me to the telephone, he took the initiative to allow me to rest while he walked her through the process, asking the questions he had heard me ask dozens of times. I wept as I listened to him taking care of her—and me.

I CAN SAY TO YOU TODAY, thirty years after my revelation as I carried the laundry up the stairs, God did indeed love Curt and Wade through me. That is the miracle that took place in the lives of my children—through me He loved them with a love that I simply did not possess because I had never known it or experienced it.

And now, when my children are grown men, I am able to hear God say, "Now, Jackie, it's time for Me to show you that I love not just your children, but I also love you."

The hardest part for me continues to be letting God into that rough and tough terrain—the recesses of my heart where jagged rocks still remain, restricting the free flow of His grace.

Pouring It All Out

FIVE

*She left him and afterward shut the door behind
her and her sons. They brought the jars to her,
and she kept pouring. When the jars were full,
she said to her son, "Bring me another one."
But he replied, "There is not a jar left." Then the
oil stopped flowing.*
(2 KINGS 4:5-6)

*T*he widow had one thing she could call her own, a little oil, and Elisha told her to pour it out. If he was wrong—if the oil didn't keep pouring—she would have nothing, and she might as well sell herself into slavery along with her sons.

There comes a time in our lives when we must choose either to simply exist in this world with our little bit of oil, or to pour it out and receive in its place the life of abundance God has prepared for us. Pouring it out, however, means relinquishing everything we have. The miracle God performed for the widow, just like the miracle He will perform for us, required commitment and action.

This is a principle I find repeated throughout the Bible as well as in modern life. When God intervenes in our lives, He demands that we engage all we have. If the widow had not poured out her oil, God would not have filled up the vessels.

Read what Jesus required of people when He offered the miracle of healing:

"Stretch out your hand" (Matthew 12:13).

"Come" (Matthew 14:29).

"Go, show yourselves to the priests" (Luke 17:14).

"Rise, take up your bed, and walk" (John 5:8).

"Go, wash in the pool of Siloam" (John 9:7).

Christ required that people exhibit their faith through their actions. His mother understood this even before He performed His first miracle. At the wedding in Cana, when the wine ran out, Mary told the servants, "Whatever He says to you, do it" (John 2:5).

Do it. A miracle requires that we *do* something so that God will work *through* us. But most of all it requires our faith. Jesus said, "If you can believe, all things are possible to him who believes" (Mark 9:23).

I FIND IT HARD TO VISUALIZE the widow standing confidently over the first large vessel and pouring with complete knowledge that the oil would flow. She probably was nervous about what the prophet had called her to do. I suspect she was like the father who brought his child to Jesus to be healed and said, "Lord, I believe; help my unbelief!" (Mark 9:24).

Faith is a gift (1 Corinthians 12:9), and God will give us more if we ask for it. I marvel at what God will do with the least little bit of faith. He never requires more faith than we have, but He always requires every drop of what we do possess.

We ask for a bushel of blessings and offer God a thimble to pour them into.

The widow had enough faith to begin pouring, and she surely was elated when the oil continued to flow, filling jar after jar. When the last jar was filled to the rim, the oil stopped. God gave her exactly as much oil as she had faith; if she had borrowed only half as many jars, she would have had half as much oil. Yet, if she had borrowed twice as many . . .

"TEXAS TEA" FLOWS

Bruce Wilkinson, founder of Walk Thru the Bible Ministries and author of *The Prayer of Jabez*, reminds us that God's miracles only occur out of our deficit. The height of the mountain of His blessing corresponds exactly with the depth of our deficit, just as the amount of grace available to us corresponds to the amount of sin. The deficit from which I had been operating was the reason I could tap in at the height I did, even though I did not understand it at the time. We should praise God for our deficits because the greatest opportunities for miracles occur when we are at our weakest.

As I have said, my deficit with regard to business expertise was total. If you had drawn a profile of me in 1979, you would have said that I was to the business world what Ellie May Clampet was to Beverly Hills. Everything she did was traditionally and socially unacceptable, but she was too ignorant to know the difference. She never knew how obtrusive she was to Beverly Hills society. Likewise, I didn't know enough about business to realize how ridiculous our model was. But in my spirit I felt God saying to me, "Jackie, you take care of My business and I'll take care

"My grace is sufficient for you, for My strength is made perfect in weakness."

—2 Corinthians 12:9

of yours." That is always His message, and He keeps His end of the deal because He knows we can't take care of His business if we're constantly worried about our own.

Like Ellie May's father, Jed Clampet, we struck oil, and that "Texas tea" became a gusher. I had started selling cosmetics in January 1979, ordering one jar of creme at a time from the home office in Dallas, Texas—sending them the money before they would send me the creme. It was a cumbersome process for filling orders, but they had never worked with a sales group with enough volume to warrant a change. By March, though, our women were selling so much, we needed products faster than the prepay method would allow. The owners told us, "When you do $20,000 volume a month, we'll get the product to you faster." Two months later, we were there, and we were growing every week.

ALL SUCCESSFUL MOTIVATION STRATEGIES

What we needed to really grow the business was training and motivation for our sales force. At least that's what the business "experts" were telling me. Magazines were filled with articles on motivation, and my mailbox was filled with solicitations for training programs. I didn't understand that language, but I believed them when they said I couldn't motivate our salespeople by myself.

A woman called me one day for an appointment to show me her motivation and training material. When she arrived at my office, I immediately had a sick feeling in my stomach. The best way I can describe this woman is "brassy." She was loud, pushy, and offensive. She spread out her material, and it screamed, "Flash and cash!" It was all about beating up the competition on my way to the top, and it was as offensive to me as she was. She explained that I could sell the material to our sales people and generate additional profit for myself. The more the woman talked, the worse I felt about her. Nothing she showed me inspired or motivated me.

She walked out, and out of the corner of my eye I saw the Bible I kept on a bookcase in my office. In my spirit I heard God say to me, "Jackie, if you will stick only to My Word for your training material, I will keep your manna fresh."

I did not know then that the motivational business was a multibillion-dollar industry, but I have since read much of the material that industry has produced. In reading, I have found that any written material that works has had its origins in scripture. God's Bible has every ingredient for success. The modern-day motivators may have rephrased it or rewritten it, but if it works, it comes from the Bible.

A few days after that saleswoman walked out of my office, Gary O'Malley, vice president of another success and motivation company, knocked on my door. Skeptically, I let him present his material. At the heart of Gary's message lay five questions:

You teach the way of God in accordance with the truth.
—Matthew 22:16

- Who is God?
- Who am I?
- Why do I exist?
- How should I live?
- What would God have me do?

Gary helped me and the women who worked with me determine our unique purpose in God, and from that moment until this day, I have never used anything but the Word for training.

All the volumes and books and tapes and seminars taught through the years can be reduced to one sentence:

Find out what people want and show them how to get it. Elisha knew that. He inspired and motivated the widow to pour out every drop of her oil, the only tangible thing of value she had, in order to achieve her vision, which was the release of her sons from financial bondage.

Everything else said about motivation is superfluous. To motivate people, we must know them at the level of their hopes, dreams, vision, and purpose. When we allow ourselves to connect at that deep level, we find the highest energy levels, most positive attitudes, and most powerful production. When we know another's heart, we automatically support it—and a supported heart cannot fail.

Success in network marketing depends on this principle. In contrast to the regular carnivorous competition in business, network marketing thrives on the understanding that giving help to another leads to the expansion of all of our territory, while withholding that help diminishes both of us. We are to become ports for one another. Just as a ship comes into port for repairs, restoration, and supplies, our lives are to be lived as ports, supplying others with what they need. And what can we give them? Jesus said, "He who believes in Me . . . out of his heart will

At the present time your plenty will supply what they need, so that in turn their plenty will supply what you need. Then there will be equality, as it is written, "He who gathered much did not have too much, and he who gathered little did not have too little."
—2 Corinthians 8:14-16

flow rivers of living water" (John 7:38). When we focus on Christ, our lives become channels for Him to pour His refreshment to others around us.

THE MOST IMPORTANT LEADERSHIP PRINCIPLE I learned is another single sentence: People will follow someone who knows where they're going. I might not have known anything about business, but my internal compass, the Holy Spirit, was guiding me as surely as the little tern follows its internal compass from its summer feeding grounds across thousands of miles of open ocean to its winter home in the tropics. I didn't offer the women who followed me the promise of wealth. Mine was a message of becoming all we were created to be and allowing the business to be a platform for that growth. When we spread that message it became so contagious that we soon had an epidemic on our hands.

Our meetings more closely resembled revivals than typical sales meetings, with prayers, songs, and testimonials. I told our sales team that if I knew business, I would teach them business. But since I didn't, we went to God for direction, and we practiced biblical principles. Network marketing is as simple as Grace Kinser explained it to me. You sell a good product, and you recruit other people to do the same. As that process continues, you develop an organization known as a "downline," choosing to earn three percent off the efforts of one hundred people rather than one hundred percent off your own.

While people in other businesses were clawing each other's eyes out to get to the top, our key to success was in our support for each other. For example, if a woman had trouble recruiting people to work with her, I would suggest, "Why don't you recruit someone to work under Jane." In other words, recruit with the intention of giving away the financial reward to help someone else. When they did that, amazing things happened. They generated momentum and confidence and soon were recruiting a large team of their own. Each of the women was duplicating herself through her recruiting—

Encourage the timid, help the weak, be patient with everyone.
—1 Thessalonians 5:14

the soul attracts what the heart harbors—creating a downline that would reflect her goals, dreams, and desires.

God often chooses women to change families, companies, churches, and nations, and our influence in these arenas grows the same way it grew in our business. Men have been given the position of authority, but I believe influence consistently yields as much power as does authority.

Biblically speaking, we see examples of women like Eve, Jezebel, and Delilah, who influenced others for evil, and others like Ruth, Deborah, Esther, Jochebed, and Mary, the mother of Jesus, who influenced others for good. There is within each of us a yearning to fulfill the function of our created design, and never more than now has the world's cry been so piercing for the influence that is ours to give.

THE GREATEST PSYCHOLOGICAL BARRIER to selling we faced was the belief that we shouldn't call on our friends, especially our church friends, when we are selling a product.

My response was, "If we're selling a good product at a fair price, our friends are the first people we should share it with. And if it's not a valuable product, we shouldn't be selling it to *anybody*."

We can't sell anything if we aren't willing to expose it to the people around us. We must share the product or message without taking offense to anyone who says *no*.

We can't let friendships be determined by who does or does not buy a product from us. That lesson extends to evangelism as well. No one will accept the message of Christ if we don't expose them to it.

TRUE BLUE FRIEND AND CONFIDANT

BY LATE WINTER 1979 WE HAD HUNDREDS more women working with us who were selling hundreds of thousands of dollars worth of product. We had no idea that the sales we generated had required a completely revamped distribution system for the company we worked for. All we knew was that we were selling a good product, having fun doing it, and prayerfully following God's lead with every step we took. We were operating out of a vision, and God was blessing us mightily.

After six months the owners recognized what we were doing and put me on a $50,000 annual salary. My delight with a salary further illuminated my lack of business acumen and my desire for the security offered by the world. That salary is a fraction of what I would have earned if I had stayed in the field and built my own organization on commission, but I didn't understand that. All I knew was that they were giving me security I had never experienced, and I took it.

I am amazed as I look back at the support system God raised around us. To this day I have never balanced a checkbook, but when the business started growing, a friend suggested that I let Ron Blue help me with my finances. I'm glad I didn't know that Ron's business was handling high net-worth Christians find ways to increase their charitable giving. If I had, I would never have walked so boldly into his office with my brown paper grocery bag filled with receipts—not just once, but every month for years. I put my bag on his desk, and he told me if I had spent too much on groceries or if a child could have shoes or if one could go to camp. I was naive enough to think that's what he did all day, and I am humbled when I realize Ron could not have shown me more respect if I had been a billionaire. He has never let me feel like my paper bag was any different than a leather briefcase.

Over time I depended on Ron for more complex financial advice for the business and for our family. When Wade turned sixteen, he wanted a car—a particular brand new car. All his life Wade had never asked for anything more expensive than a new pair of football shoes, but he presented a persuasive case for this new car. (I should have recognized then that he was destined to become a successful attorney.) I didn't know if we could afford a new car, so I went to see Ron. He bypassed the financial questions, asking instead why I wanted to buy the car for Wade. "Is it because you feel guilty?" No. "Or because you think his self-esteem needs to be built up?" No. "Or because of your own pride in being able to buy it?" No. "Then why do you want to buy it for him?"

Tears welled up in my eyes when I said, "I think it's just because I want to thank him for being a partner with me and for all the ways he has helped me."

Ron smiled and said, "Then go write a check for it."

Good, But Not the Best

SIX

She went and told the man of God, and he said,
"Go, sell the oil and pay your debts."

(2 KINGS 4:7A)

T he widow had more than just jars full of oil. She had God-made oil, and God makes only the best. In New Testament times, when Jesus turned the water to wine, the ruler of the feast tasted it and said to the bridegroom, "You have kept the best wine until now" (John 2:10). Of course it was the best—better than anyone had ever tasted because the Master Himself made it. Likewise, the miraculous oil God made for the widow must have been the finest anyone had ever seen. Elisha immediately told her to get rid of it. Otherwise human nature might have led her to regard that beautiful oil as the end itself rather than the means. After all, it had come directly from the hand of God. We have a way of turning God's gifts into idols—worshiping the gift instead of the Giver.

The day came when I had to recognize the idols of my heart. I realized I had made idols of God's finest gifts to me—my sons. I came to understand that human idols have only one purpose, to fall off their pedestals, and I repented and relinquished them to God, so I could worship only Him.

God told Abraham to take Isaac to the altar not because He needed Isaac, but because He needed Abraham. In the same way, He needed me to give up my sons to Him and realize that when God created them and entrusted them to me, my job was to be obedient and sensitive—to mold them in the way He had already bent them, but with a clear understanding they did not belong to me.

In a similar way I realized I was worshiping my business and the security it provided. I had put God's gift to me in its own high place and turned it into an idol.

After ten years in cosmetics sales, our group out of Atlanta was doing 82 percent of the entire company's business. My compensation included use of a company owned house and car. Never had I felt so secure. When my sons graduated from high school, one enrolled at Vanderbilt University in Nashville, the other at Emory University in Atlanta. I was proud of them and pleased to have been able to provide them a fine education.

Then a consultant from a top accounting firm told the company owners that my sales group controlled such a large percentage of corporate sales, that if we ever decided to leave and start our own competing business, they would be left holding the bag. The consultant had no way of knowing that I was too naive to have entertained such an idea.

God chose the foolish things of the world to shame the wise.

—1 Corinthians 1:27

But the owners responded to his concerns. Up to that point they had never told me anything about how I should operate our part of the business; now they allowed the consultant to draw up a list of rules and regulations.

It didn't take long for me to realize that from a practical standpoint these guys owned me—lock, stock, and barrel, because by this time, they owned my house and car, and they fully controlled my paycheck. I had placed too much of my security in the company that supported me. I had to know to whom my soul belonged; only then could I be free to succeed without questioning my own motives. I had to resign.

It's frightening see how the devil offered me a counterfeit to keep me from recognizing God's highest and best. He convinced me that something quite good was really the best. His method so often is to creep up on us unawares, and before we know it he's hidden a little jar of lust here, a bit of jealousy there, a bottle of pride in the corner—all disguised as "good" things. But God always points out the truth, and He gives us an opportunity to act.

I went to Ron Blue and laid out the facts, and he confirmed my decision to leave. At the same time, he insisted I write down my reasons for leaving, then store the list away. One day, he said, the devil would make me question my decision, and I needed to have my reasons on paper. He reminded me of Habakkuk 2:2-3, "Write the vision and make it plain on tablets, that he may run who reads it. For the vision is yet for an appointed time; but at the end it will speak, and it will not lie."

The decision to leave was more about my perception of what the company was doing than about the company itself. From their perspective, they were rewarding a successful generator of sales. But to me, the strings attached were too many and too strong. I could have stayed with them and remained financially secure, but I could not allow them to be responsible for me. I had to pour out my dependence on anything or anyone but God.

I was reminded again of the rich young ruler. Jesus didn't need that man's money. He needed the man's complete reliance. I was at the point of becoming addicted to my beautiful home and car and salary. My security controlled me.

Our God is in heaven; he does whatever pleases him. But their idols are silver and gold, made by the hands of men.
—Psalm 115:3-4

I wrote my letter of resignation, and the owners tried to convince me to stay, but I did not. I walked out of the house and into a rented apartment, gave them back the Mercedes, and took money out of savings to buy a used Chevrolet. My sons came home from private universities and finished their studies at Georgia Tech and the University of Georgia.

I never felt as free as I did when I refused to allow the fear of losing my security to control me. I could never win until I was no longer afraid to lose.

The "Dingbat" Years

The husband of one of our saleswomen owned a Fortune 500 financial services firm, and for years he had tried to recruit me into his company. John had seen our success in cosmetics sales and thought the same skills would translate into success in his industry as well.

I never took his overtures seriously until I was suddenly without a job, and I accepted his offer to become a senior vice president managing stock brokers in fourteen states. If starting out in business the first time was my Ellie May Clampet chapter, working in securities was my "I Love Lucy" chapter. Lucy was more sophisticated than Ellie May; still she put herself into situations way beyond her abilities, with disastrous results. I knew I was in trouble almost immediately when John said one day, "You'll need to go over to Emory in a couple of weeks to take a little test." That "little test" was the Series Seven examination for stock brokers, one of the toughest tests devised for any industry. I didn't know enough to understand the questions, much less the answers, and I flunked. Nothing I had done had prepared me for the financial aspects of the securities industry—and the securities industry is all about finances.

For ten years in cosmetics, everything I touched had gone right. All of the sudden I was in the opposite position. Nothing went right. Even the janitor knew more about securities than I did, not to mention the men with twenty years of experience who now reported to me. They nicknamed me "The Dingbat Out of a Jar of Creme," and that's exactly what I was. This dingbat did learn one thing, however. God knows that just as nature needs seasons, His children need seasons of success to build confidence and seasons of failure to put us back in touch with our humility, lest we take ourselves too seriously. (I wish I had learned that lesson before I took a bathroom break at the seminar where I was speaking and reappeared with the hem of my full skirt and slip caught in the waist of my sheer-to-the-waist pantyhose!)

Specifically, my job responsibilities included sales and compliance, which meant making sure none of the brokers did anything illegal. Today every brokerage office has its own compliance officers, yet here I was responsible for a quarter of the nation for our company.

On my third attempt, after weeks of study, I passed the Series Seven examination, although I'm still not sure how. Finally I could concentrate on what I did best—identify and recruit good people and encourage them to do their best. I realized then that John had been right about one thing—many of the principles that led to our success in the cosmetics business did translate to securities.

In the securities business, as in network marketing, you don't hold a paycheck over anyone's head. You can only encourage people to reach their own goals. The root of the word *encourage,* "cour," means *heart.* At the deepest level, when you encourage a person as the prophet encouraged the widow, you give them heart. You give them courage to operate from their deepest place, bypassing superficial motivations and mountaintop experiences that are so soon only history. You don't seek revival-type euphoric "commitments" that are only a memory when the sun rises the next morning. When you encourage people you seek the deep seat of their emotions—the cellular memory of the heart.

For four years I recruited people to be stockbrokers and encouraged them to operate out of their vision to achieve their goals. Throughout my tenure at the company, my group's sales numbers were near the top when compared with other regions. But the grind of the compliance responsibility wore on me, and I was glad when John sold the company, allowing me to leave without being a quitter.

MIDCOURSE CORRECTION

I had known for years that I wanted to have my own network marketing company where the wealth would be shared with the blood equity of the field force. Too often in network marketing companies go out of business because of the greed and egomania of people at the top. While in the securities industry I had developed, along with three friends, a product that we were excited about launching, and the sale of the securities company seemed to bring about the right timing. Just as we were about to launch, my friend Ann Schoenberg invited me to an meeting hosted by National Safety Associates (NSA), a network marketing company that sold water filters. I could not attend, so I asked my son Curt and his wife Lori to go in my place. Curt was in the commercial real estate business at the time, and Lori commuted to downtown Atlanta for a full-time job. When they heard about the company and the product, they decided to join NSA. A few weeks later I met the company president, Jay Martin, and he asked what it would take for me to make a full-time commitment to NSA.

My response was, "As soon as I'm convinced that NSA will be around for my grandchildren, I will make that commitment." I did not yet have grandchildren.

After I investigated the product, company, and marketing plan, I realized this was the place where I could accomplish my goals of an international distribution system without the financial liability of owning a company and without the administrative and inventory responsibilities that were not my forte.

I had never planned, or even thought about, having a family business, but here Curt, Lori, and I were, working together. Three eager Beavers became four when Curt's uncle, David Beavers, joined us a couple of months later.

I soon realized that a family business strengthens both the family and the business. The beginning of the industrial revolution, which brought workers off the family farm and into the factory, coincides with the beginning of the breakdown of the family as each member headed in different and unrelated directions. Likewise, in the corporate structure people exit over conflict; in a family business they hang in and resolve conflicts. That's where character is formed.

Our business not only has the strength of family ties,

but the knowledge that comes only from experience. Curt knows more than he knows he knows about network marketing because of his early exposure and participation. As a teenager he was handling inventory and shipping long before he had any idea of the success he would enjoy in the industry.

They say everything in real estate is location, location, location—everything in life is relationships, relationships, relationships. In the end all that matters is what we pour into them and what they pour into us. This principle is demonstrated in our business, where the majority of our volume is generated under three women who started out with me twenty-five years ago in the cosmetics business. Another significant portion comes from a friend I worked with in the securities business, and another from a family friend whom we've known for more than forty years, who carried our business into Europe. With the help of them and others, we have recruited, trained, and support distributors in more than twenty countries with over $100 million in sales.

THE MOST IMPORTANT RELATIONSHIPS in the success of a company are those between the leader and the people working with him. In thirty years as founder, president and chief executive officer of NSA, Jay Martin, because of his willingness to pour, has helped his industry make a different kind of midcourse correction. Jay has taken the "skim-scam" out of network marketing by underpromising and overdelivering. He has replaced hype and smoked mirrors with science, technology, and integrity. With a proven product he has produced a world class company in which every individual is expected to pour for more.

A number of years ago a book titled *Heroes* claimed, "We no longer have heroes cause we no longer need them." A more recent *Fortune* magazine article said, "If we no longer have heroes, perhaps it's because we no longer recognize them." September 11, 2001, brought revival to both the need and the existence of heroes.

Perhaps we have overlooked those heroes who build companies and businesses that allow us to make a life as well as a living.

"I load sixteen tons and what do I get? Another day older and deeper in debt." That song of the 1950s reflects even more today a people unable to *be* because they are consumed with survival. I salute the heroes who have the courage to step up to the plate and make it happen. In 1936 Henry Farley wrote a book *The Good Society* in which he dreamed of a society where the ancient traditions of brotherhood loyalty and honesty are consistent with the abolition of poverty and the development of wealth. Jay Martin has accomplished that in a business context. I have consistently seen him treat people in a more Godlike way than any church I have ever been in. He is honest with people and loyal to a fault. People perceive the company as a family where they are trusted and supported. That is the secret of the success of his industry.

Chronos and Kairos

SEVEN

*"Pay your debts, and you and your children can
live on the rest."*

(2 KINGS 4:7B)

*T*he widow hoped for enough to pay her debt, but God gave her so much that she and her children could live off the proceeds for the rest of their lives. God is a God of abundance. He never gives us almost or just barely enough. He stands ready to share "exceedingly abundantly above all that we ask or think" (Ephesians 3:20). He is a limitless source as long as we do not place limitations on Him by telling Him not only what we need, but how He should provide it. Notice that the woman never answered Elisha's question, "How can I help you?" Rather, she made herself and her sons available to receive God's blessings.

Too often we do not make ourselves available. I heard an old story about a woman standing on the side of the road with a heavy sack slung over her shoulder. A man driving a wagon offered her a ride, and she climbed up in the back. After a few miles he looked back and the woman still had the sack over her shoulder. "Ma'am," he said, "why don't you put down your burden?"

Cast all your anxiety on him because he cares for you.
—1 Peter 5:7

"Oh, no," she said. "You've given me a ride. I couldn't possibly ask you to carry my burden too."

God's Word in the Greek text uses two words for *time, chronos* and *kairos.* Too often we are like the woman with the burden, living day to day, watching the clock and refusing to release our burdens to God and make ourselves available to receive His blessings. He wants us to be like the widow, giving our burdens to Him so we can accept His gifts of abundance.

THE BURDEN OF MY LIFETIME—the one I tried so many times to give to God but kept taking back—was my relationship with my parents. My father lived eight years longer than the doctors had expected, and during that time I prayed that he would not die until our relationship was healed.

We needed some special time together—a kairos moment.

The boys were grown and gone, and my father and mother had been living with me for five years in the same one-room fishing cabin the boys and I had escaped to years earlier. (After we moved out I renovated it and expanded it for my parents, then moved in with them to help take care of my father when he became ill.) The years were difficult, as I still harbored anger and resentment for their treatment of me as a child.

My father was near death when I ordered a tape from Focus on the Family about father/daughter relationships and the need for reconciliation to allow the child to go on. I hoped the tape would open the door to a conversation that would lead to our reconciliation.

A few weeks after I gave my father the tape, I walked outside the house one day and found him sitting on the deck. He asked if I would sit and talk with him. I did, and we experienced the completion of our relationship that I had longed for. He asked me to forgive him for not protecting me from my mother and for his physical abuse of me at her demand. He assured me of his salvation and filled in some of the missing pieces from our past, including the abuse my mother had experienced as a teenager.

111

Later that day as I was preparing to leave town on a business trip, I remembered Sunday was Father's Day. I gave Dad a special gift and a card thanking him for all the things he had done for me.

I left the next day for a trip to Memphis. That night I dreamed of my father's death and funeral. Two days later he died. The father/daughter tape was running on the tape player in the room with him at the time of his passing. Only later did I realize my *chronos* timing was off—Father's Day was the *next* Sunday. But if I had waited until the right day on the calendar, I would have missed a wonderful *kairos* moment.

A FEW WEEKS AFTER MY FATHER DIED, I was on my way to a spiritual renewal weekend where watches were not allowed, and the battery in my watch literally stopped. God knew what I didn't: I was in bondage to the clock. He knew that I would sneak a peek. From that moment I understood that this particular weekend was a divine appointment. I still laugh at God's sense of humor in His dealings with me in that incident. I also weep at His intimate knowledge of the depth of my soul, and I celebrate His enduring mercy in my life.

Of course, I was not alone in my bondage to time and my frenetic pace. Every day we Americans demand more out of every *chronos* minute and avoid opportunities for *kairos* moments. We've learned to live out of our heads and not out of our hearts because it hurts less to think than to feel.

On my way to the retreat the *chronos* on my watch stopped, but *kairos,* God's season in my life, was picking up speed. I was moving toward a time of listening and hearing Him say that it's okay to feel pain. Jesus did not run from His pain, nor should I. To be in touch with my feelings means that I peel away all the layers of self-protection I laid across my heart for years.

For some people that peeling process might take years, but apparently I'm not like most people. My heart's protective layers got ripped off all at once, laying my heart bare in front of more than a hundred people. I had attended a fund-raising dinner and was listening to Tom Grady, president of Grace Fellowship Counseling Center in Atlanta, deliver the message. Tom grew up on a farm in Iowa, and when he was a boy his parents promised a sheep dog for his birthday. The dog was to be a fine pedigree and quite expensive. Tom eagerly awaited his birthday and his dog, often musing over their anticipated friendship. Finally the dog came and Tom was able to see and touch him. The dog was even more beautiful than he had imagined, with papers that would have impressed the queen.

But when Tom tried to love he dog, the dog did not respond. Weeks passed, and instead of growing accustomed to the family the dog became aggressive, and finally vicious, toward people and the other farm animals. Try as he might, Tom could not calm the dog. Eventually this beautiful animal had to be destroyed.

Tom's father offered to buy another dog, but Tom refused. The experience had been too painful. Then on a cold winter day Tom spotted a pitiful stray dog that somehow made his way through the snow despite ribs protruding from starvation, a broken leg, mange that had left him with large hairless patches, and an oozing sore. His ears drooped, his head hung, and his tail was between his legs. Obviously near death, the dog would not come when called, so Tom fixed some water and food and carried them far from the house where the dog would eat it.

He's talking about me, I thought as Tom talked. *I'm the stray dog in the story. On the outside I look like that other fine dog—I work hard to maintain the appearance of a fine pedi-*

gree—but deep inside I'm that stray dog that no one could possibly love.

The next day the food was gone, and the dog was still there. Tom repeated the feeding process, each day bringing the food closer to the house and talking to the dog more.

God has given me the bread of life and water from the eternal well, I thought, and I could feel the tears welling up in my eyes.

After several days Tom was able to touch the dog and put salve on his sores and splint the leg. Eventually the dog came to the house for his food, with a bowl of his own and a bed that had been put on the porch next to the warm chimney. In a short time "Blaze," as Tom had named him, gained weight and seemed almost well. His hair was growing back, his tail was wagging, and his ears stood straight.

That's Jesus comforting me with the balm of Gilead. God has set a place for me at His banquet table, and Christ has placed His robe of righteousness on me. All I have to do is receive the love He offers. I don't have to earn it or deserve it any more than the dog did. With that realization my tears flowed, and despite the comforting words of the people around me, there weren't enough napkins in the room to dry them.

My tears were tears of joy, and in God's *kairos* moment He had given me the lesson of His love for eternity.

THE FINAL YEARS WITH MY MOTHER passed with difficulty as I—by now a grandmother myself—continued to try to earn her love. She was totally dependent on me for her survival, and her words and actions indicated that she totally despised my being. Our relationship came to a head when I returned from a three-week conference and she was more abusive than ever.

"From this day forward," I told her, "I will take care of you, but I will no longer take your abuse."

I had never spoken to her like that, and she knew I meant what I said. Our relationship was never good, but it improved to some degree, aided by the positive deposits she was able to make in the lives of my children and my grandchildren. They hold memories of her rocking chair and her "world's best" biscuits and fried chicken, and none of that could have happened if I had abandoned the relationship.

Mother was eighty-two years old when she went to the hospital for the final time. She lived her last seven weeks there, with me in her room most of the time. I cannot explain my desire to be with her at the end except through God's grace allowing me the privilege to spend those days with my mother without being overwhelmed by resentment. I believe she experienced God's grace in those days as well, for it was the first time in my life she was not in combat with me.

Death has been swallowed up in victory.

I was in the room with her when the doctor stood over her and said, "Mrs. Knight, this is Dr. Lynch. Do you hear me?"

Where, O death, is your victory?
Where, O death, is your sting?
—1 Corinthians 15:55

A slight movement indicated that she did.

"I have some important things to say," the doctor continued. "I rarely do this, but if you have any relationships that are out of order, with God or with anyone, you need to take care of them."

Later that night she was awake, and we talked. Only in her dying was my mother able to forgive me for being born, and for the first time in my life she asked me to forgive her. I told her I did, then she told me she loved me, and she professed her faith in Christ. My final time

117

If anyone has caused grief . . . you ought to forgive and comfort him, so that he will not be overwhelmed by excessive sorrow. I urge you, therefore, to reaffirm your love for him.
—2 Corinthians 2:5, 7

with her was our only *kairos* moment together. In that ever-so-little time together we were able to grieve our profound mutual loss.

The Final Quarter

It has now been fifteen years since my watch stopped. Those years have consistently increased my ability to hear and sense God's *kairos* timing. What I see now in the lives of my sons and their families is exceedingly abundantly more than I would have known to ask or think. Survival was as far as my mind could stretch, but they have already entered into His rest, living not out of the love of power, but the power of His love. They understand that life is not intended to be a buzz saw, but rather an opportunity to use their resources to accomplish and pour out to their purpose.

I continue to marvel at the ways God takes care of me. Whenever I stand in a grocery store line with my buggy overflowing with food and extras for my grandchildren, I am reminded of His faithfulness to me. I no longer worry about whether I have enough money in the bank to cover the check. The income from our business has given me the freedom of time and money to pour out in greater measure. I am pouring into my grandchildren as my grandmother poured into me, seeing firsthand how in families, as in network marketing, the real benefit becomes apparent in the second and third generations.

Knowing that God had redeemed me and my family, I was ready to take my rest as well in the final quarter of my life. Then, after I told my friend Art Powell about my discouraging report from the doctor, he said, "You've reached the place to which we all aspire—you have achieved yourself out of a place. You cared for both of your parents until their death. You saw both of your children achieve interdependence with you. The same is true in your business and your ministry. You have duplicated yourself in such a way that they will continue without you."

I knew he was right in confirming my readiness to cross the finish line. Should I have been surprised, then, that my body responded with cholesterol levels that would soon lay me in my casket? In nursing homes—and outside of them, too—people die when they no longer have something to look forward to.

Then God used my good friend Julia Kelly to hit me in a blind spot with His Word. With courage and love she told me I had allowed the sin of fear of growing old alone to become the stronghold in my life. She reminded me that perfect love casts out fear, and God's love for me is perfect. Yet another friend. Patty Davies, added, "Jackie, that extra weight working against your heart is the spirit of heaviness being reflected in your body. The spirit of praise is the solution for heaviness."

I considered their thoughts as I began to write this book and realized that for the first time in my life I can release the emotions I had bottled up all my life. Everything up to now has been about survival. Now my survival demands something different. Henry Wright, in his book *The More Excellent Way*, explains what medical science is coming to understand better every day: When we become host to negative emotions such as anger, fear, and jealousy, our body responds by releasing toxins that lead to disease and, ultimately, death.

I am only now dealing with the effects of actions I took and pain I endured decades ago. When our family was in financial crisis, I had no time to process my feelings any more than you would think about the mortgage payment when your car was skidding off the highway. Life is difficult, and it is said that the denial of that fact is the root of all mental illness. I didn't deny the fact as much as

I ignored it and did not deal with its effects.

I thought that by now I would have eliminated fear, anger, and perhaps even sin, from my life with God's help. I have not.

The good news is He has given me a new set of opportunities, and by addressing the emotional issues I have ignored for six decades, I am pouring out the poisons that would send me to an early grave. I am reenergized for the final laps and eager to see what God has in store for me.

NEITHER RETIRED NOR RETARDED

At grandparents day at my grandchildren's school, I saw a letter that one precious child had written about retirement—except he confused the word *retarded* for *retired*, and described all the ways his grandfather had changed since he moved into the big brick house behind a gate with other retarded people. I decided that I would be neither retired nor retarded. Instead, I would enter a new season where Christ would allow me to pour out more.

I suspect the widow with the oil did not live the rest of her life in retirement, choosing instead to tell the world of God's abundance in her life. She who had chosen to bring her difficulties to Him through the prophet not only experienced a miracle, but after thousands of years she continues to pour her light onto the paths of pilgrims in progress.

I choose to follow the examples set by the two women who influenced me most, my grandmother and Grace Kinser.

My grandmother was still pouring in full measure until she lay down for a nap one afternoon at age ninety-seven and didn't wake up.

Grace inspires others years after her death. In fact, I have decided to live like Grace lived and to die like Grace died, going to a party wearing a red dress, with a box of brownies on the front seat beside her. On her way to the party she stopped for gas, witnessed to the attendant, then stepped out of the car to make a telephone call. There she had a heart attack and died. The attendant came to her funeral, where he was saved by grace.

Grace Kinser saw life as George Bernard Shaw had, not as a brief candle, but as a splendid torch to be passed on. Her children and grandchildren take that torch out to the world today.

I now understand that life is not a sprint, but a relay. A track coach instructs runners that passing the baton smoothly is even more important than raw speed. It's not about how much I can accomplish in my lifetime, but how I can pass Jesus on to the next generation. I feel great joy when I see that my sons have embraced with tenacity the love and the values I poured out to them, and they have married women who embrace those values with equal tenacity. They will go further in their lives than I came, and my grandchildren will go even further.

But the "next generation" doesn't stop with my sons and their children, for if we do nothing but lead our children to Christ, we have only replaced ourselves. I hope God gives me as long as He gave Mama Harris—thirty-seven more years to pour myself out and let Him refill me. What an opportunity! I refuse to spend those years "retired," playing golf or bridge or gazing at the horizon. I'm going to follow the track coach's other bit of advice and "run through the tape." The runner who slows down before reaching the finish line loses the race.

Tragedy of life is not dying, but dying not having poured out what God has poured in. The Apostle Paul told his spiritual son Timothy, "For I am already being poured out as a drink offering, and the time of my departure is at hand. I have fought the good fight, I have finished the race, I have kept the faith" (2 Timothy 4:6-7). The apostle had poured out his entire life for Christ, and now he needed to see Timothy. "Be diligent and come to me quickly," he wrote.

Paul had some more pouring to do.

So do I.